SIGN POSTS

A COLLECTION OF ESSAYS

Volume VI

Other Books by Don Davison

An Outline of a Philosophy of the Consciousness of Truth
The Concept of Personhood in the Evolutionary Process of Being
The Game of Life: A Player's Manual for Executives and Others
Sign Posts: A Collection of Essays, Volumes I–V

Poetry

Thoughts and Feelings Book I
Thoughts and Feelings Book II
Needles from the Ponderosas at Zirahuen
Seeds from the Ponderosas at Zirahuen
Pitch from the Ponderosas at Zirahuen
Humus from the Ponderosas at Zirahuen
Sawdust from the Ponderosas at Zirahuen
Sun's Rays Bouncing off the Ponderosas at Zirahuen
Shadows Beneath the Ponderosas at Zirahuen
Cones from the Ponderosas at Zirahuen
Pollen Sifting from the Ponderosas at Zirahuen
Reflections from Lucerne
Searching Swamps
Questions
Time's Echoes
Memories
Insistences
Splashes
Ripples
Pebbles

Collections

Always Extolling
Murmurings
Iris and Other Things
Pieces of the Journey
Through the Swamps of Time
Reflections from Lucerne
The Twelfth Hour
Pebbles on the Shore
Still Water

SIGN POSTS

A COLLECTION OF ESSAYS

Volume VI

Don Davison

Zirahuen Publishing
Flagstaff, Arizona
Contact the author at
DrDavison@pathtotheself.com

ISBN 978-0-9858130-5-5

Cover photo and author photo by Patricia Davison

Special thanks to Louella Holter, and to Tina Rosio, from W.

To Patricia, for everything.

This collection is also dedicated
to the United States of America

A Litany for Freedom

All of Don Davison's books have water on their covers. Water is one of the most essential attributes of the planet Earth; without it, life as we know it would not exist. It deserves our most considered attention.

Davison's collections of poetry all end with "Finding Pieces." Many of you have asked, where did the rules for the Game of Life come from? They come from many places and different times. Good hunting!

CONTENTS OF PREVIOUS VOLUMES

SIGN POSTS I

A Human Face—A Human Touch
A New Point of Departure
A Word About Politics
Grow Up, America!
Immigration—A Brief History
Iraq—The Last War
Self-Love
Thank You, Artists!
The Mediation of Reality
The Past—Present—and Future
The Person
Wars of the Moment
What Is Right?
An Agenda for Us All
The United Nations

SIGN POSTS II

Vignette
Sufficient Security
It's Free!
The Ethics of Politics: An Oxymoron or Truth?
Democratic Oversight
Health Care
Our Current Moment
A Question for Our Times
We Need Enough Truth to Know the Truth
Procedural Questions
Understanding Our Current Moment
Standpoints and a Methodology for Dealing with
Postmodern Perspectives
Damn It! I've Had Enough!
Take Courage, America!
How Much Is Too Much?
The Truth—Elections—and the Health of a Nation
A Humanistic Manifesto
Splash
A Beacon on a Hill
All Hands on Deck!
Learning to Die Well
My Current Status Is …
A Direction

SIGN POSTS III

While We Are At It: Health Care 2.0
Kudos and Thank Yous
Economics 101
Time, Place, and People
The Gift
Obama Got Most of It Wrong
The Paparazzi
A Streaming
The Greatest Challenge of Our Time, Part 1
Fear, Facts, and Ideologies
The Coming Revolt
Thinking Matters
Globalization
We The People
Trust
Let Me Speak!
The Greatest Challenge of Our Time, Part Two
History Does Not Run Backwards!
Cultural Blinders
Human Life Is a Moving Force
Come to the Party!
A Visit with the Dancing Muse
Bite the Bullet!

SIGN POSTS IV

Sandbox Syndrome
A New Transparency
A Note to the Maryland State Employees,
to Wisconsin State Employees, and
to All Local, State, and Federal Employees
Changing Our Minds
It Is Deeply Troubling
A Question for Our Times
End Game
Entertainment Is a Strange Bed Partner
How Often Do We Need to Be Reminded?
In All of This ...
Justice
Nothing Is Free!
One Wonders
The Arrogance of Tyrants
The Drivel Called "News"
Where Are We?
Who Said That?
Media's Gift
Food for Thought
Derivatives
Frustration Reiterated
Looking for That Thing
Our Time
So Politically Correct
Now Wait a Minute!
We Are a World of Laws
Freedom of the Spirit
An Observation
A Perfect Storm
I Am an I Am!

SIGN POSTS V

The Greatest Challenge
The Facts at Hand
Immigration
Not a Mandate
It Was Predictable
O Ignorance
Dedicated Ignorance
Ignorance—Again
Image and Likeness
Today's Moment
Almost …
The Multifaceted Diamond
Some Women's Vote
United We Stand—Divided We Fall
Facts
Now Is The Time!
The Great Wound
The New Age of Transparency (and our
Current State of Cultural Affairs)
A Person
Truths at a Blink
Always Hope
The Idiocy of it All
The Three Musketeers
The Facts of the Matter
Polling the Youth (On Matters of Importance)
Just How Smart Are We?
Marriage
What Legacy?

A Glance at the Past—A Peek at the Future
Messages
It Has Been Said
Perpetrators
Always Walking—Always Running
Advice
Epitaph
Decisions
Choose!
Life
What We Must Know, We Must Be (Part One)
To Dream

CONTENTS OF THIS VOLUME
SIGN POSTS VI

Honor and Dignity	1
A Matter of the Utmost Importance	4
The U.S. Debt	7
Take Heart	9
What We Must Know, We Must Be	11
To Dream	14
Beware	15
Lucidity	16
Notice: Someone Said	17
A Person	18
A Caution	20
Opportunity Presents	21
The Failure of the Wrong Man	23
Whose Is That?	25
Our Now	28
The Last Straw – Impeachment	29
Worth Remembering	32
The Emperor Has No Clothes	33
The Dam Has Broken	35
Ruminations	37
Where Am I? Where Is It?	39
What to Do?	40
What Will Win?	41
A Life	42
God's Soul	43
Beware These Times	44
The Pendulum Swings	45
Learning to Learn—All Over Again	51
Always Hope	54

Manners Matter   55
Obama Redux   56
Homage to Louis L'Amour   57
Truth, Facts, and Spengler   60
Why Is It That …   63
A Perception of Our Place in Time   65
Thank You Obama   69
Baltimore   71
The Baltimore Syndrome   72
How Important Is This Moment?   79
A Brief Afterward   83

AUTHOR'S NOTE

I am primarily a poet; these essays are intended to help "flesh out" various themes and topics found in my poetry. Where I feel it is appropriate, I might refer you, dear reader, to a particular poem that further elucidates certain thoughts or sentiments. If not otherwise noted, such inclusions are my own work.

Sign Posts are collections of essays written to shed some light on my personal thinking. Over the years, students and others have asked that I write some small pieces on what I felt about this or that, in an attempt to share some of the fundamental points of departure that have guided my thinking and stimulated searching in my various fields of interest. These pieces are augmented with new and intriguing ideas that I find as I continue to discover the richness of the human garden and the unfathomable depths of the human experience.

I believe that "as a species, we must act in love (in that Frommian manner: with an active concern for all life and growth) by operating and proceeding with knowledge, care, responsibility, and respect while we dedicate ourselves to growth as self and circumstances change. We must live with the awareness that a sanctifying process is always underway" (from the essay "A Word About Politics," in *Sign Posts I*).

I have a tremendous amount of compassion for Barack Obama. His personal circumstances growing up were difficult. As I have said elsewhere, his abandonment by his father and then his mother were trying enough. And then, to be fed an ideology of social poison when he was young served to create a social myopia that has not served him well. While gifted with sufficient athleticism to be able to enjoy sports and an intelligence of some stature, he has failed to integrate into his intellect the insights of the ages—those problematic and stellar pieces of history, those of thought, word, and deed that shed light on the personal journey of us all. I can only hope in his later reflective years that he can come to grips with the lost opportunities that were his to contribute quantum leaps to the social well-being of nation and world. He and his family will remain in my prayers.

FOREWORD

The greatest current challenges for our democratic republic are religious and educational. A participative democracy needs an informed populace—and a motivated one. To be straightforward: we need a citizenry that is smart enough to vote and committed enough to be present in all things. Let's all do what we can to help each other become informed enough to maintain our freedoms by shouldering our personal, social, and governmental responsibilities.

The themes of the day are complex and extremely important; among the most outstanding are deficit spending, legislative agendas, immigration, appropriate military response, loss of freedoms, and clean water. (As noted above, all of Dr. Davison's books have water on their covers.)

When I comment on the foibles and the greatness of history, my emotions run the full gambit. And yet, I always try to consider the beneficence of a beautiful life for each and every human soul.

I have tried to write the essays in the multiple volumes of *Sign Posts* in such a way that there would be no need to "read between the lines." I'm not sure that I succeeded. Perhaps that is why I have never abandoned poetry.

HONOR AND DIGNITY

Does honor follow dignity, or dignity follow honor? We must know there is that reciprocal of truth that sheds its light on the human path and illuminates our actions. Facts are facts and for the most part are self-evident from our bank of common sense. Square pegs in round holes only fit if the peg is smaller than the hole. The arches of the corners—those supporting architectural and linguistic necessities that give strength and meaning to the whole of our cultural and communication infrastructure—are a part of what is too often missing. In this we must remind ourselves that lies are of two kinds: omission and commission.

Honor and dignity, those standard-bearers of the ages, are currently missing from the lexicon, and therefore from our understanding of the day. We stumble over ourselves when we attempt to use the word *respect* in places where it does not fit. "I respect the office but not the man" is an oxymoron. The "office" is the activity of a person and a group of others (the administration). History speaks for itself in all of its splendor and horror. It is indeed true that only the truth can set us (U.S.) free. Before that can happen we need to be able to comprehend the truth. What is it? What does it look like? Taste like? Feel like? Sound like? Smell like?

It is not without reason that we describe the stench of corruption and the abundance of a lack of common sense. We know something is missing—in fact we know a lot is missing from the words and deeds of the day.

1

It does not take a genius to know when people are lying. If their words and actions do not follow, something is wrong. The impossible is a felt problem for most. Right and wrong is also self-manifest for most reasonable people.

So how can we be sure that we demonstrate the honor and dignity of our words and actions? It really is quite simple— integrity is the only thing that presents and maintains its presence over time in thought, word, and deed. And while it may take someone some time to comprehend whether something is true—remember Hands up! Don't shoot!—it does not take forever if we choose to really know and reflect on what it is that we are thinking about and sharing with each other. And think also of those apologies that can only come from maturing souls who choose to be free enough to act with integrity and be honest with the facts at hand.

We can learn from Nature that the rhythm of reality from which we operate, live our lives, is a constant flowing of a chain of events, some over which we have quite a bit of control, some over which we have very little control. Yet it is also a fact that sufficient control can be had for most of us to mature into participating members of a society. This is a control that demands a reciprocal action/responsibility component. If this was not the case, we would be living in a constant state of chaos. But this is not the case. The pervasive cognitive activity for a maturing individual is the perennial perspective of "if–then," which is a fundamental building block of reality. Most of us go about our daily living without experiencing a continual onslaught of catastrophes.

Words have meaning and actions have consequences. Converse with a commitment to the truth and act accordingly. That age-old adage—"My word is my bond"—is such a simple manifestation of a way of living. It is unfortunate in the post-postmodern world that simple truths conflict with the "image" problem. So many lost individuals spend their days and nights attempting to come from some safe place where they mirror the deficits of understanding that is reflected in much of our adolescent culture. If we could operate from a biblical perspective of "created in an image and likeness" of a divine process, we would also operate from a deep and abiding sense of integrity and consequently we would all be much better off.

A MATTER OF THE UTMOST IMPORTANCE

Reading tea leaves can be a simple pastime. Divining the psychic concerns and motivations of a diffident and fluid culture at the whole and its parts, or at least a critical mass—a boiling point—is not an easy thing.

We set upon our daily tasks and seldom do we turn our attention to the circumstances of our country's woes. In any case, we don't wonder too much until something really big, different, disastrous, comes our way and even then we try to slip it into some reasonably comfortable place and continue on our individual paths.

Only every now and then does something scratch our sensitivities sufficiently to garner more than a passing glance. This current moment is one of those times. How many of us would have thought that what is now occurring in the Middle East would have presented itself in the twenty-first century? When did we ever consider trillions of dollars of debt? Or, when did we think we would get so little from the three branches of government?

We had some vague notion of a Democratic Republic in which shared powers were established to iron out differences and solve essential problems. Stasis and petulant behavior were not things we equated with the growing needs and aspirations of our beloved country.

Stupid is defined as being astonished or struck senseless. One cannot operate in this state of being. These stupefied individuals, in their ignorance, are not contributing to the well-being of the whole. The clock is ticking and time is being lost forever for everyone. We only need a sufficient number of honorable courageous souls who seek the salvation of the country—a country that has the potential to offer a sanctuary for all those who are willing to try.

We have now reached a point where our President and Congress, and at times the Supreme Court, have delivered less than acceptable actions.

We have some necessary choices to make: We need to participate in our own well-being and assist in the well-being of our great nation. That we are in trouble is obvious. That too little has been done, and done frivolously, is also obvious. Waiting for last-minute resolutions, budgetary and otherwise (read "deals"), is a pathetic way to run a country. The world is not some second-rate used car lot. We need transparent agreements drawn up and agreed upon by reasonable minds.

Any president who releases war criminals—some, if not many of whom will return to the battle field—is unfit for office. This arrogant disdain for advice and cooperation is one of many current hallmarks of incompetency. This is not what we expected, or deserved.

We only need sixty-seven votes to impeach. And this is not a red or blue thing; it is an American thing. We cannot and should not wait while people die as this country flounders domestically and internationally. The truth has been apparent for some time: This president was not a leader, is not a leader, and never will be a leader. He is unfortunately an incompetent in his current office, and in the parlance of the military, he is "unfit to serve." Articles of impeachment have already been drawn up and are available to any and all who wish to read them. There is more than one, and any of them would offer sufficient reason to impeach.[1]

Present the articles and vote. Whether we can agree on all charges is beside the point. If we can agree on any one of them, it is sufficient to impeach and move on. We cannot afford the time and treasure to wait, nor can those who perish in the global circumstances, hoping and praying for us to get our act together. We owe this to ourselves, our loved ones, our country, and the international community.

What a powerful message we would send to our allies as well as our enemies. In the midst of the ongoing prattle, we would say with the strength of truth, "You no longer represent the office sworn to uphold the Constitution of the Republic." And to those Democratic and Republican patriots, and there are many, who are finally willing to acknowledge the accumulation of the facts and can choose the greater good for our nation, we say, together, that because we have to begin from where we are, parties and politics, you will not be opposed in the upcoming elections. Those of you who choose not to stand for the salvation of this nation will all be fair game.

We must turn this corner and reestablish the integrity of our governmental process. In one fell swoop the credibility of the Congress would be restored. Open the gates of freedom and purpose by stopping all this nonsensical and destructive political correctness. In one move, recapture the commitments to life, liberty, and the pursuit of happiness.

We have sufficient information available to us and we need to act now. Get it done!

THE U.S. DEBT
(Two points of view)

"Look at how many people we have helped!" (Served, thus generating dependency.) Every coin has two sides: to lie by omission is still a lie. This leads to one or the other (class warfare), a yes and a no. You can't have both and grow.

"Look at how much freedom you have stolen!" Should not our objective be to honor each and every one, to the degree that we and they are able? Freedom is the essence of one's self-expression. It belongs to all of us (as our responsible commitment to self and to each other). "Love thy neighbor as thyself." Simply put, this means to love one another. This leads to a reciprocity that synergistically benefits us all—a yes, yes, and yes again.

Which world would you prefer to inhabit?

Let's be candid. (How I hate that word! It approaches too close to candy: sugar-coated everything.) So, let's just be honest—not as a request but as an emphatic command. Integrity speaks for itself just as the truth speaks for itself: If true, then true. What part of this do we not get? But ... It's just ... Well ... Probably ... Maybe ... Anyway[2] ... are all words that bespeak an avoidance of the truth. Shifting feet and stargazing are not what this country needs.

We cannot wait for two more years to remove this president. Time waits for no one—not the United States, or ISIS, or anyone else. We must impeach immediately and send a clear message to all the citizens of this great republic and the rest of the world: Not now—not ever!—will we allow another neophyte, much less an arrogant prejudicial adolescent to inhabit our White House, and to gather a gaggle of same-minded adolescents and incompetents to staff his administration.[3]

There is reciprocity in physics that speaks to a plus and a minus—zeros equal zeros. I took the 3:10 to Yuma, and for those of you who wonder, and for those too young to know, the older version is much better—the one with Glen Ford and Van Heflin. Let's get honest and save this wonderful Republic.

TAKE HEART

Who bears the burdens of our times? Certainly not those who've gone before—their time was theirs, whether alone or together.

There have to be some intelligent people in all of this. I've seen their tracks, read their words, felt their presence, been inspired by them and the fortitude of their commitments.

The heart must hold firm the spirit and the body, with that courage so essential to our journey. We must be the lion-hearted defending the pride, to be all for one's own self, and one's own, in that natural reciprocity of nature. Everything is connected to its purpose.

For too long many of our brothers and sisters have looked outside their selves and fashioned pseudo-selves on whims of adolescent projections, those half-baked dreams and inspirations that, when done well with the maturity of time, leave tracks for others who will have challenges of their own.

The headwinds are beginning to blow; waves are coming in greater numbers. Swells are deeper, feeding those reflective reposes so necessary to understanding. Crests are higher, from which we see those treasures of well-being lying at a distance. The shifting of a critical mass is bringing to bear a new consensus, a consensus that demands that we all speak with one voice: We will forever be responsible, individually and as a nation, for allowing incompetence to prevail in our elected officials.

9

There is now, beyond any shadow of doubt, a history of abject trifling in offices of power and responsibility. Those who do not see or cannot understand are either blind, stupid, or both. No matter what their predilections for one ideology or another, there is simply no excuse for the citizenry to allow incompetence to run rampant in the various branches of government.

It will be some time before relationships of mutual trust and respect can be reestablished with the international community. This is as it should be. We must regain our own self-respect and demonstrate a will to follow through with our intentions and responsibilities. This is what maturing adults do.

WHAT WE MUST KNOW, WE MUST BE
(Part Two)[4]

With our innate awareness of our knowing, our "here now," being becomes concomitantly a belonging not only to the "One" but also to each other. "We are too much the same to have so many differences."[5]

Teilhard de Chardin,[6] it was thought, in speaking and writing of the noosphere, was describing the coalescence of thought and thought sharing (perhaps the Internet "netting" the globe). He seemed to call it the Christic Presence, in that mystical body sense. I think he was speaking of each person, each mega molecule, rubbing/touching shoulders in a real sense with another mega molecule, another human being. I think he was referring to the shouldering of the movement of humanity, of the new implosive centripetal movement of the entire human species; we are one and we can choose to live on the edge or in between the center (urban) and the edge (rural)—but we cannot choose honestly not to be a part of the whole.

A case can be made, with the technology of the day, that there is no longer any "edge," and yet there is still, in the sociobiology of the now, an obvious orientation that has a different sense of touch and relationship that is exuded by people who have historically been raised in the urban and rural environments. And it must be noted that it is not only the proximity of many of us in closed space, it is the distinct lack of a daily communal interface with the entire surrounds of nature that creates a void in the thinking of many of the people of the day.

11

There remains a disconnectedness, a lack of connecting—despite the phone companies and the Internet marketers encouraging us to "reach out and touch someone," telling us that a better life is "just a click away," or that it takes "just a swipe to get there"—this just doesn't get it done. If we "lose touch" we lose our self, that most essential "quickening," that soulfulness that opens the opportunity for us to grasp the fullness of the abundance of nature itself. Love is much more than a word; it is dedicated activity, an existential "all-touch" that can get everything done.

There is in the history of philosophy that parsing of our thought and that focus on "the thing in itself"—*das Ding an sich*—when indeed it has always been a "more than," a participation in a "divineness" that is inherent in all of creation, a mirroring of the completeness, of the effervescence of existence itself.

As we continue ascending, we find ourselves always on a new threshold encountering a deeper and more elegantly meaningful understanding of ourselves and our surrounding circumstances. As Teilhard said:

> *Seeing.* We might say that the whole of life lies in that verb—if not ultimately, at least essentially, fuller being is closer union, union increases only through an increase in consciousness, that is to say in vision. And that, doubtless, is why the history of the living world can be summarized as the elaboration of ever more perfect eyes within a cosmos in which there is always something more to be seen … To see or to perish is the very condition laid upon everything that makes up the universe, by reason of the mysterious gift of existence.[7]

In all of this I am reminded of the transitions of thoughts to words and feelings to words. For example, words such as translucent, transcendent, transparent, transposition, and transubstantiated can all be seen as moving from an awareness of light to a creation in light.

Our current moment is full of thoughts and feelings that are groping, in intended and unintended ways, attempting to grasp the significance of our presence in the commingled presence of others, of another (an other). We seem to be approaching a grand crystal staircase wherein lies a spectrum beyond spectrums by which we ascend to some new space–time in which we experience, enjoy (in joy) the omniscient.

TO DREAM[8]

"La vida es sueño y los sueños, sueños son."
(Life is a dream, and dreams are only dreams.)[9]

I dreamt about a new skin/membrane,
a multipurpose-universal,
internal-external,
concept-fabric
that is intrinsically interactive –
protective – open.
A responsive, living
(and I know that is redundant)
holographicness,
that is efeta stuff,
where IT-WE
is always becoming I-WE
and love-life prevails.

BEWARE!

The post-postmodern quandary occurs in the ripening of a moment when the disconnectedness of the species is accentuated (because of sheer numbers) and separation is brought about by advances in technology, specifically in the arena of communication, and as a result, a lack thereof.

From phones and cell phones to "text images," "images," and "text me!" the machine "reaches out and touches someone" by vibrating, jingling, screaming, or bashing, and attempts to communicate with very few written letters that, while they possess a shadow, sometimes of sentiment, most often are cryptic vestigial remnants of an interchange, a there-there as opposed to a here-there. We might even ponder on the word *crypt* with reference to humanity itself.

On the other hand, a message with the human voice and that wonderful repertoire of subtle and not-so-subtle non-verbal cues offers a larger vista for our mutual understanding. If we choose to isolate ourselves, we are losing contact with ourselves and others. This cannot be a good thing for a social anima whose primary motivation is to love one another as one loves the self.

LUCIDITY

An appreciation of life always starts, for us, from where we are. It already is. It always will be. This we know: the cycle of birth, life, and death is a never-ending saga. The eternal and omnipresent challenge is to live with a set of sustaining values that honor the truths of the ages and the truths of the now in a complementing synergism.

Fear of nature, of the dark other, of the unknown others who are similar but different—fear of the emerging self and the free sharing of that self with the process of creation—is not a prudent standpoint.

No man is just who you think he may be behind the pen. There are always those primeval traces that course through his veins and affect the screens of the eyes and the mind. And there is that cauldron from which boil and splash his emotions, fed by fires within that rage and subside and rise again like the rising and the lowering of the tides. And yet, at times, there is that other admixture of faith and hope, commingled with charity that bubbles forth from the end of the searing pen.

NOTICE: SOMEONE SAID

"We (in the United States) have a myopic hubris that sours our personal dispositions and contaminates our foreign policy. We are blinded by it to such a degree that—in due course—we lost our way, we became 'ungovernable.' We extinguished ourselves. We did not keep faith with our inheritance. We squandered the crop and turned our back on truth."[10]

There are many ways to describe our current moment—the above is one very passionate example—and there is truth in what he says. We have failed our country, we have failed ourselves, and we have failed our children and grand-children. It is now up to us to take on this dishonest adolescent (President Obama) and to obstruct in every way we can, every second of every day, his efforts to destroy this wonderful nation. The battle cry of freedom must continue to ring from every nook and cranny. Let's get it done!

A PERSON[11]

A person,
an image and likeness,
presents itself.
What constellation of events
makes a person a person?
Time and space surely play a part –
history wraps its arms around our knowing
(being)
and we are caught in those
tumbling times from which we come.
The events of the ages adhere and dispose.
Myth and legend merge from learned stories
and surge to the forefront
of our selected druthers:
Choices!
Always choices!
Heroically we attempt to justify our beliefs,
beliefs that we employ
to weigh and measure
those choices,
our choices,
choices that have bloodied the earth,
maligned our souls,
torn asunder relationships of family,
and of love,
and as well,
inspired our heroics.

* * *

Why is it that in the face of difference
we resort to modes of being
that do not complement the needs of the human family.
What cursed daemon
sits upon our right shoulder,
what gargoyle perches upon the left?
Why in the face of nature's benevolence
do we insist upon wallowing in chaos
when we all stand in wonder and awe
at the birth of a child?
Simple truths befriend us all.
To these we must adhere,
to these
we owe an everlasting thankfulness.
Nature's profound mandate:
– Pay attention or die! –
must be met with a
chorus always singing,
"Yes to self! Yes to life!
Yes to all life!"

A CAUTION

When the change from Democratic Party as a descriptive term to Democrat as a noun was made, the political battle was lost—when the single word was adopted as the Party of Choice, the war was lost. And when the good use of the word liberal was high-jacked and thrown into the fire and forged into "Liberal," the truth was consumed in the flames.

We must always consider the Spanish phrase: ¡Poderoso Caballero es Don Dinero! (Powerful Knight is Sir Money!) Always beware current times and the media of the day. The rush to the airways with video, audio, and print versions is often done with little, if any, forethought or investigation. Therefore, it is incumbent upon every individual to be their own fact checker.

If you are going to choose to believe anything, you must own the truth of what it is that you are living your life by. You must tie it to yourself with the tentacles of history and one's own historical experience. Always ask yourself: Does this complement human life, all life?

OPPORTUNITY PRESENTS

Too many Republicans have lost their moorings and have no grit. Most Democrats have learned to group like rats and have gathered, mired in their own muck.

Where can we find those men of virtue—from any Party—those stalwart patriots who have the courage to step to the podium and say, "Not now, not ever will another time come when this great country of ours will lose its way like it has in these last few years."

We know the Constitution has been trammeled by a president, an administration, and an adoring media, all of whom have completely lost their way. We won't—we can't—just wait for the Supreme Court to act—they too have made their mistakes.

What we need now is a group of solid soldiers, those who know right from wrong, who know that Fifty Shades of Gray refers to seasons of life, and that they can never be co-opted by Hollywood. Those shades of gray belong to the few tested souls who know and love what this nation has stood for and still stands for: life, liberty, and the pursuit of happiness, with the blind lady meting out justice.

Their time of adolescent rampaging must come to an end. The adults in the room, and those gifted younger folk who yearn for what they thought might be lost, must see the light. It is still shining yonder over that next rise, that hill, that next mountain.

Never quit! Never give in or give up! Take the reins and bring this wagon 'round and head up that trail where that shining light still shows the way for us, for them, and for the rest of the world. We all need to bind up our wounds and face the future together. It will be tough enough with the perennial resurrections of old evils that will always continue to try the souls of us all.

Now is the time: Impeach and move on. Contrary to the lazy thinking of the day, we don't have time for any part of the current nonsense of those who won't join the new revolution, the one that will take us up that hill to liberty's mansion. Our house is cluttered and dirty, downright filthy, with the stench of ignorance, arrogance, intransigence, corruption, and lies.

We need to start at the top and clean out the White House and move right through to the bloated and misguided bureaucracies and floundering festering enclaves of evil "civil servants."

Enough of us now know how wrong much of what has happened has been. How gullible have we become? How foolish have we let ourselves and our neighbors become? Stop the foolish and stupid behavior. The time is now!

THE FAILURE OF THE WRONG MAN

The current president—a constitutional scholar he is not!—
doesn't have a clue as to the spirit of the law—that which
comes before the law, binds the law, directs the law, that
which embodies the strength and depth of purpose for a
religious adherence to the law.

He is an immature ideologue who fancies himself important, as all adolescents do. He is an unfortunate individual
short-changed by his own parents and compromised by
others. He is not stupid, although a case could be made for
his ignorance.[12] He just shined up to a slick veneer of
words—platitudes—that spoke in a simple tongue to those
less acquainted with the foibles of history.

Those who listened and gobbled up his porridge were less
prepared than most to make the difficult journey into
maturity. They saw only government control and largess as
fundamental to their well-being. They knew nothing of the
eternal thrust of freedom with concomitant responsibility, a
responsibility that bespeaks a follow-through that accom-
plishes the protections of greater freedoms leading to a
deeper growth in understanding, one that adds stature to a
person, a culture, a country, a world.

He was sidetracked as a youth, and in his fear-drivenness
he stubbornly disregards the facts at hand and so flounders
through his life, leaving behind a wake for others to clean
up. Along the way he despises the Constitution and those
who would most benefit from its purpose and intent.
Mouthing blather he rapes their souls and steals their

freedom. He violates their sensitivities and takes pride in being fawned over by those less fortunate. He truly is "an enemy of the people."

He cannot assume the mantle of a dictator. His crimes are obvious. His importance is only to serve as a lesson for us all: Beware the amateur! Impeach him now before the diaper overflows at a cost of even more trillions of dollars and more precious time to clean up the mess.

Everyone has equal rights under the Declaration of Independence and the Constitution, but none of us are "equal." We are all unique personal gifts from One to one to be shared with another. We can dream our dreams and exercise our freedoms to try and accomplish those dreams. There are no guarantees—just an infinite array of possibilities stacked against a lifetime. And that is all any of us ever have to call our own.

When will the children who serve in Congress—and other branches of government—stop simply dancing around the mulberry bush? The individual freedoms so necessary to responsibly owning one's self cannot be secured by such children (all children lie). We continue to be plagued by the festering ignorance of the species. We must enter upon a new enlightenment that touches everyone.

When will sufficient integrity, purpose, and virtue finally rise up to admit and confirm that this is the wrong ideology, wrong man, wrong time, and wrong place! The time has come to impeach and move on. This is an imperative. We cannot wait for two years. A message must be sent to any and all that this will not stand.

WHOSE IS THAT?
(Why there is so much self-inflicted ignorance.)

When a culture isn't prepared to answer fundamental questions—like the title of this essay—there is a high probability that it will spiral downward out of control. The control we need, of course, and of which I speak, is self-control, that essential and miraculous maturing sense of oneness that gives to those who fathom its importance a maturing measure of self-responsibility.

The grand "it" or "them" of which so many speak is that burdening "secular other" that becomes for many their constant psychic companion, an omnipresent direction of their thinking that leads them to a historical syndrome that has petrified and putrefied individuals and cultures for eons.

Our current iteration is the euphemistic "blame them" with the mental, emotional, and spiritual modus operandi that is so much a part of the current mind-set of the protracted adolescent thinking of the global culture of the day. The United States is a quintessential example of this and it pervades all levels of the culture.

It is with pen in hand and hope in the heart that I take this opportunity to elucidate and hopefully shed some light on this debilitating malady.

We, the rational social animal, the homofaber, the destroyer, the symbolizing, freedom-aspiring, soul-seeking, sentient being operates from a template of habitual behavior based upon a perceptional intransigence. This has led us to the adoption of a nihilistic creed that says, "That's just the way I am!" as some sort of unreasoned mantra. A spontaneous self-imposed epithet that demeans our very being and becomes a part of our social intercourse, adding yet another layer of supposed commonality to our "protective groupiness."

In this somnambulance of adolescence, as we commiserate in our ignorance, we say, "So many do it (say it). So it must be true. Everybody does it." This ought to lead us to a distressing thought: That so many are caught in this stasis, when Nature's law says, "Pay attention or die!" Maintaining a fidelity to a lack of growth does not bode well for anyone or anything.

This perspectival error, when knowledge, care, responsibility, and respect are the signature of maturing human thought and interchange, must be turned away from the flippant rhetoric of the day to mirror a profound awareness of an emergency of being. Life, by virtue of its existentiality, is that sacred nowness that honors its own presence and purpose.

Stop the thoughtless contrived diatribes of ignorance! Rise up and confront the current stupor in which we act as if we have forever to own the truth of life! We must manifest that holy commitment to the sanctity of all life.

We must be about a courageous act of faith that takes us toward a new baptism of self-confirmation, a confirmation that says "Yes!" to the All of life.

How can this be done if we objectify our descriptive thinking in such a way as to eschew any reflective thought that could lead us to responsible actions that give us a measure of redemptive behavior of the parts and the whole?

The venue of our actions must be that individual and communal hand with which we touch each other in loving ways in thought, word, and deed by clipping the wings of this rambunctious human paradigm (by untutored thinking, by saying too much, and by doing too little). We must, instead, focus our thought—guard our speech—and do that which is essential and complementary to our well-being.

It cannot be that the sloth with which we watch the current tableau of our machinations is sufficient to give to the young, or to anyone, a new template of a renewed religiosity that harbors sufficient love of self and others to carry us beyond our current malaise. This is a malaise that has us ensconced in an inability to correctly/honestly own in an appropriate fashion the salvation of our kind. The hour is late. The existential challenge is before us. Stop the dithering, the wallowing in an effete political correctness, and do the right thing!

The answer to the question of the title of this short essay is: "It is mine and it is mine now!"

OUR NOW[13]

If one does not have a religious commitment
to one's own life,
there is no lasting fundamental commitment to any life.
Out of the fatigue of time
– from the wavering luminosity of spirit –
come the images of those who have gone before,
those who will come after.
It is for all of the intrepid souls,
those who have gone before
steadfastly into the winds of time,
that we are obligated to do our very best
in everything we do.
From what deep well of soul scratching
will sufficient courage surge up to do the right thing?

THE LAST STRAW – IMPEACHMENT

When a coalescence of the will of the people manifests itself in a rising tide of awareness and commitment, we will hear a crescendo saying, "No more! Not any longer!" But many citizens are not yet sufficiently informed to participate responsibly in the care and maintenance of a republic.

When maturity responds to an actual chronological age, when in human history an organic sense of growth and awareness becomes a part of the psyche of a culture—great things can happen. We, the United States of America, are on the verge of that very moment.

Enough has become "Enough!" Enough people have realized that while being an angry adolescent is a part of our natural history, we cannot tolerate having those qualities manifested in the highest office of the land. And when that office is occupied by an individual who is guilty of high crimes and misdemeanors—to wit, stealing freedoms of expression and accomplishment from those he has sworn to protect and defend, and bearing false witness to the citizens of this great nation and the world through lies of commission and omission, as well as treasonous disregard for the sacred founding documents—we are morally, practically, and politically obligated to act.

There is the dawning of an awareness that we (many of the citizens of this great republic) did not really understand what Barack Obama was really saying, much less intending to do to our beloved country, so that we were ensconced in a stupor of acquisitions, malaise, and yes, a naive sense of political correctness (now that is an oxymoronic phrase if there ever was one). However, we certainly do now have sufficient information with which to respond to our current circumstance. And this response must come with some dispatch. Our nation is teetering on the brink of dramatic and fateful change, a change that will bring untold suffering to millions, even billions of people who believed in and aspired to the possibility of living in and creating a government "of the people, for the people, and by the people" by giving their just consent to be governed by an enlightened and committed president who has sworn to uphold the Declaration of Independence (that sacred document recognizing inalienable rights to life, liberty, and the pursuit of happiness) and the laws of the Constitution of the United States of America.

That the process of impeachment should begin immediately is beyond question: The thefts have occurred and the lies have been told. We cannot continue in an ignorant state of "wait and see." We are fundamentally obligated to protect ourselves from the oppression of tyrannical behavior—for this we fought the Revolutionary War, for this we have maintained a commitment to the founding documents of this nation. We must act now. We cannot just hope to take more seats in the Senate in the next election, thinking that then maybe we can stifle his headlong plunge into national and international disaster.

All life carries with it an existential mandate: True, mine, now! And as the old famous phrase says, "Now is the time for all good people to come to the aid of their country!" We must not only remove the malevolence of thought, word, and deed from the office of the president and his administration, we must send a clear message to future generations who must assume an informed and protective posture in husbanding this nation's resources and protecting the rights of liberty.

Likewise, we need to send a clear message to the despots of this nation and the world that we will not tolerate malfeasance from anyone, much less elected officials. We must remember that we are a nation founded upon principals of freedom and responsibility, and that those attributes of being are paramount to maintaining the great gifts of our founding forefathers and foremothers.

WORTH REMEMBERING:

Sometimes the beautiful is apparent
– to those who wish to know it.

Wouldn't it be nice if we could all remember the stirring words from those perspicacious "others" who have passed our way? Such as Martin Buber:

> Speechmaker(s), you speak too late. Just a little time ago you would have been able to believe in your speech; now, you no longer can. For, a moment ago, you saw as I did, that the State is no longer led; the stokers still pile in the coal, but the leaders have now only the semblance of control over the madly racing machines. And in this moment, as you speak, you can hear as I do that the levers of economies are beginning to sound in an unusual way; the Masters smile at you with superior assurance, but death is in their hearts. They tell you they suited the apparatus to the circumstances, but you notice that from now on they can only suit themselves to the apparatus—so long, that is to say, as it permits them. Their speakers teach you that economics is entering on the State's inheritance, but you know that there is nothing to inherit except the tyranny of the exuberantly growing It, under which the I is less and less able to master dreams of that over which it is the ruler....
>
> Economics, the abode of the will to profit, and State, the abode of the will to be powerful, share in life as long as they share in the spirit. If they abjure spirit they abjure life.[14]

THE EMPEROR HAS NO CLOTHES

Obama is losing it. His futile attempts—and those of his supporters—to justify their juvenile actions (read not well thought out) are rapidly becoming pathetic, downright incompetent, not only with Obama's complete lack of leadership but also for his supporters who are pushing back against the truths of his bunglings. Do we see a whirlwind of behavior that cannot stand the light of day?

Their reaction to this incompetence is a loud and pathetic "No!" At first just breathed under their breath, barely audible, and then an audible that slowly becomes a screaming of that single word, "No!" In that finality of realization that they have been wrong all along there is an agony of heartfelt desolation, of abandonment. They all thought he was so "one of them"—one of those who finally "got it," one sympathetic to their errant particular and universal worldviews.

After all, adolescents don't want to be embarrassed. However, with the mounting body of "action/no action," really wild gesticulations and silence, they find the nonsensical delusion of their voting position untenable.

The first response has been a pushback on the unfolding evidence as it accumulates with the passage of time. Just saying something louder and more often will never correct the sins of the past. Eventually it will become increasingly difficult to support those standpoints as other truths become known. Then the embarrassment will be too great not to support the enlightened facts as they continue to unfold.

33

This pushback-denial, then skepticism, and finally accept-ance mirrors the age-old progression of adolescent to maturing young adult and then finally, as one continues to grow, to a maturing adult who has a better grasp of the truth and who owns the truth of the now in the now. There will be a sickening realization that time waits for no one and that in order to be present in their now, they must adopt a more cogent perspective on the real. We won't be waiting on any apologies; we will be too busy undoing the morass of mistakes.

THE DAM HAS BROKEN

While it is rewarding to have written some social and political criticism that was "Spot On!" I find it puzzling and a little aggravating that it has taken so long for others to come to see and understand more of our current political missteps and weakened efforts.

I offer the following from George Steiner's 1961 work, *The Death of Tragedy*. May we mine the depths of those truths so essential to our freedoms.

Words carry us forward toward ideological confrontations from which there is no retreat. This is the root tragedy of politics. Slogans, clichés, rhetorical abstractions, false antitheses come to possess the mind (the "Thousand Year Reich," "Unconditional Surrender," the "class war"). Political conduct is no longer spontaneous or responsive to reality. It freezes around a core of dead rhetoric. Instead of making politics dubious and provisional in the manner of Montaigne (who knew that principles are endurable only when they are tentative), language encloses politicians in the blindness of certainty or the illusion of justice. The life of the mind is narrowed or arrested by the weight of its eloquence. Instead of becoming masters of language, we become its servants. And that is the damnation of politics. Corneille knew exactly how this process takes place. No dramatist is his equal in rendering the "feel," the complication, and the cancerous vitality of political conflict. Only Tacitus can rival Corneille in showing how men are embedded in the constricting, mind-clouding matter of political circumstance....

The characters assume abstract positions and abide by them to the point of ruin. Their free will is mastered and corrupted by political rhetoric....

The evil of politics lies precisely in this separation of the human person from the abstract cause or the strategic necessity....

When rulers begin talking of "streams" and "things," humanity has lapsed from both their language and their intent.[15]

* * *

This also attends to the "politics" of the Supreme Court and to those men and women, those civil servants (who are anything but civil or servants) who have sworn to uphold the founding documents of this noble republic. These documents are some of the finest ever produced by the mind, heart, and hand of the species called Humankind. Still we trifle at the peril of losing their significance and the freedoms of our souls.

RUMINATIONS

We have arrived at a place where some pseudo erudites concoct their own brand of "right idea." There are those who choose to wallow, those who seek in the adolescent projections of their current moment some "dispassionate" expression of a "reasoned" statement: "All or none!" We hear what has become the hue and cry of those who have yet to seek sufficient equanimity birthing magnanimity.

With text after text, we see the sloshing-over of gratuitous adjectives—self-selected from some effete "almost there" position of those who would have the great journey of life be some communal cradle that continuously rocks us into insensibility.[16]

They lie! Or they muddle in some romantic pasture from whence they gaze into the sky looking at the clouds. It is prudent to recall those famous words from La Celestina, "Sin embargo no son las mismas nubes."[17] (Without a doubt they are not the same clouds.) They are certainly not those of our youth.

We need, in parsing the thinking of any age, to "stand still in silence, so that we can hear (see/comprehend) the truth of the now."[18] We need to saturate our ruminations with a healthy dose of those eternal truths, those truths written on the bottoms of our feet; we are the Peripatetic who, from history's wanderings and wonderings, must give to the ages, to each and every one, those many-faceted diamonds of our experiences, of our understandings, of our deepest fathomings.

We cannot hope to converse without such understanding. We must instruct to those eternal hominid standpoints so that when new and awesome knowledge breaks upon the shores of our "new-nows" we can take sufficient time to reflect and draw some measure of understanding from our long, perilous, and miraculous sojourn, those Pearls of Great Price.

The power of reflection allows us to fix our values and to maintain a fidelity to those that we consider our core values. Included among these are the choices we make to change our mind about our history and the way we interface with the real world. This process leads us to deepening self-ownership and provides continuous opportunities to exercise personal responsibility as it relates to the freedom of personal and social growth.

A poetic relationship with our memories, our perceptions of reality, and also our dreams, provides a cementing exercise that creates a template for an appreciation of our own lives, of all life.

WHERE AM I? WHERE IS IT?

We delve into delicious flights of fancy.
Imagination opens its doors and we risk it all.
The savory freedom of others'
purpose and intent
grabs our souls and we succumb
to a search for hidden treasure.
What great needs bend the iron of our hearts
and take us into realms wished for,
hoped for,
sought after?
How is it that a vision so clear emerges
from the turmoil of reality
and settles in tranquil reveries?
And why is it that a gentleness
covers everything,
hard or soft?
Lost upon a range of fertile vistas
we gladly spend our hours hiding
from God's plan,
or is it when we are so enthralled
that we find ourselves strolling in His Garden
in misty mornings and dappled afternoons?
Are these the times when we vaguely see
through the thin film of the present
and gaze upon eternal truths
that light flames birthing dreams?

WHAT TO DO?

So …?
While riding the synaptic bull,
leaping hither and yon,
jabbing a pointed finger
in this eye and that,
we're catching a case of
Blame Them,
anything, anyone.
Choosing in the now to own one's drift
while cursing history's depths of efforts
is a pitiful pastime.
There is the challenge:
to wait for no man or beast.
To seek nothing is abominable.
To this
I prefer the existential quiescence,
embracing in exuberant passion the all of life,
while leaving a trail
next to the barefoot tracks
of St. Francis.

WHAT WILL WIN?

And so … you ask,
What will win?
To you and all others
I say,
Have you not felt that sigh?
It comes upon exiting
those wooded and marbled floors
of those grand apocalyptic agoras of our day,
where merchant-dice abounds amidst
the glitter of light and mirrors and glass,
when finally our feet touch the earth.
When enveloped in the brilliance of the day,
drizzle of the season,
darkness of the night,
our assaulted senses
in a holy expiational exercise
(those brief reposes given by life's moments)
– again –
smother us in fleeting quiescence,
sending rippling through our being
a symphony of biology
resonating with ourselves.
What will win?
Life will win!

A LIFE

The myth of politics in the moment
is defined by the whole
as it wobbles on and off course
in some self-serving, self-caring trajectory
of space/time.
The assumption:
a party makes a difference.
The truth is,
it is what's really right that matters
and this is the individual,
either in itself
or in its commitment of another to others.
We all measure time in a lifespan of one.
So ...
then it must be that each and every person
is precious,
worthy of every effort
to make of themselves what they can.

GOD'S SOUL

The grand measure of God's Soul
is that in the coalescence of the universe
His heart beats again,
and in this thrown-ness into freedom
choice defines our souls.[19]

BEWARE THESE TIMES!

There are sufficient truths in the peaks and valleys of history. Our challenge is to ferret them out and to share the richness of those truths with the world.

* * *

"England, too, discovered the ideal of a Free Press, and discovered along with it that the press serves him who owns it. It does not spread 'free' opinion—it generates it."[20]

"The (Whig) Party agent Dodington described his parliamentary activities in these words: I never attended a debate if I could help it, and I never missed a division that I could possibly take part in. I heard many arguments that convinced me, but never one that influenced my vote."[21]

THE PENDULUM SWINGS

Someone has already said, "It must be important, he said it twice." (From the movie *Bite the Bullet*.)

The current moment mirrors a previous moment—"How long GW, how long?" (From the movie *McLintock*.)[22]

When and where will we find enough honest people to articulate the facts at hand? Does life mirror art or art mirror life? There is a synergistic reciprocity that feeds upon itself.

In all of this, cultures surge on and the individual flows back and forth with the tides, always looking for an eddy— a calm-water moment to catch one's breath, to reminisce, to wonder.

Coincidental happenings grab our attentions, and for brief sheltered seconds we think we possess some understanding of life's purpose, we think we have insights that give us an anchor. Then we come to know: A person's life weighed out in pieces of silver becomes a measure of one's humanity, governed by an incomplete economic circumstance.

Obama's attempt at psycho/emotional/spiritual surgery was ideologically infected and did not heal well. His election was the single greatest political mistake ever made in U.S. history. He is a kind of rapist—he takes sacred personal gifts of freedom from those who cannot and have not yet learned to possess their freedoms, those who find ways to make themselves dependent upon the largess of a government. In this way he rapes the truly innocent and the aggrieved. You cannot commerce in life and death.

In his misplaced messianic hubris, he believes that what he does is good for everyone. What childish logic concludes that one size fits all and less freedom makes one feel more secure? And he is not alone in his lack of commitment to those founding documents that birthed this nation.

Ignorance is alive and well in both parties—as both infiltration and institutionalization have spoiled the soup, and so it is with an ignorant and lazy citizenship. The nation is losing its ability to own the truth of its birthright, and its very purpose for being. Word and reality connect the dots of truth—call a bastard a bastard—and don't get caught in some naive idiocy and think of circumstances of birth. This is a reference to the bastardization of behavior itself towards humanity itself—against the very nature of our species, of those endowed with certain inalienable rights, those of life, liberty, and the pursuit of individual happiness.

There is a difference between someone who knows they are being raped and someone who only recognizes the rape in retrospect and then becomes aware of just how much was lost.

As candles flicker in the sanctuaries—and candles flicker in all of the nooks and crannies of the sacred spaces of the world—one may ask, how many candles? You may ask, and I will tell you, more than you could count in a lifetime. How will we ever know then? Well now, we could try to imagine all those flickering candles or, we could light our own candle—and share its light with the world. Nature, of which we are all an integral part, has always cried out to us,

"Pay attention or die!" Lest we become seduced to malaise, beware and remember: "As it was in the beginning, is now, and forever shall be."[23]

The adversity of the age presents itself along with the eternal gifts of the ages. It is with our current moment that we all begin. Questions come in moments of adversity, and we wonder: Is there, could there have been a better, a more efficient way to learn what we need to know? Yes, there could have been. And yet, the serendipity of the struggles helped give insights that we otherwise would not have had. This makes it now our responsibility to own those insights.

Who among us possesses beliefs that turn the rights of people on their head? Sharia Law recognizes some human rights—but not all human rights. Our issue is with that part that dehumanizes humanity itself: No freedom of religion, no freedom of conscious choice, and gender discrimination.

The iron fist of history or the running water of time are both baptisms in a religiously cultural sense, offering an opening that must be traversed with dedication. It is always the case that the old world passes away and a new world comes into being. "And I saw a new heaven and a new earth: For the first heaven and the first earth were gone and the sea is now no more."[24]

Form dictates content and it all starts for you and me, all of us, with the self, with one, and a choice of that one to do what is perceived to be in its and its loved one's best interests.

To touch is to communicate. To know someone, to be a friend with someone, is essential. To know one's own self is paramount. To become sufficiently endowed to stay the course of giving the gift of one to one as one shares the self with others along the way is the only fully human path. Protect the Pilgrim Road! To hold fast to the Rules[25]—to live them, to hold another's hand, to walk some distance with another while one coincides with the One, to be in that silent presence, listening to another—that is the greatest of gifts.

The pendulum never swings twice in the same direction before it swings in the opposite direction. If there is an attempted counter-swing, the follow-through's swing happens in its own context.

Say what you want about the United States of America. Have we sinned? Who hasn't? Have we made mistakes? We have never sat down. We have grown into a union and we have saved that union time and time again.

We will not languish in our mistakes. It may take us some time to sort out our problems, but eventually we will, and we will remain committed to our founding principles. This we also know: deep down in our souls we will have to revisit those founding principles, we will have to embrace them over and over, again and again. We will have to teach them to our progeny. Such is life's way.

Grinding away, albeit with a demonstrated passion, on a formulaic moment—who, where, how, rags to riches, poor me, poor you—could be problematic, could be a place that is not in our best interest. How we go about living our lives makes us who we are today and tomorrow.[26]

There are many and myriad ways of finding facts. The problem is to be able to make sense of them. What do we do when we cannot understand those pesky facts at hand?

Some of us just ignore them, some just give them a tired glance and move along at their own harried pace. Few grab them and wrestle them to the mat and finally give them that 360° turn to see if they fit the template of common sense. In most cases we don't need a "head of the pin" focus; some practical standpoint will do.

Take for example the current U.S. debt of more than eighteen trillion dollars. Anyone with even an ounce of sense knows that this is a really big number. They also know—even if they have paid only passing attention to the facts of the day—that this number now surpasses our entire yearly gross domestic product. How stupid can politicians and citizens be? It has become perfectly clear that many people of every ilk can be very stupid in their wanton avarice, sloth, and ignorance.

We might say that as the pendulum of human behavior swings, these are those human moments, when forgetting (ignoring) simple truths, we all act like lemmings. "Group think" sweeps the field and we choose ignorance in the face of the facts at hand. Just because others say it, or do it, does not mean that it is in the best interests of anyone. Always take a moment to reflect upon the information you are choosing to "upload" to yourself and for others. It may be an unbearable load to carry. And now, there is also what the Old Monk would call "Saint Google's hoard of information."

It is of value to recall that events always conspire and make of a significant number of those so entangled what they really are in times of need and deed. When we really find ourselves otherwise engaged, we are presented with opportunities to own the mettle of our souls. Now is that time; now we have that purpose to which the winds of time and change have brought us. Behold the sacred mantle of free-dom. Behold the souls of us all. Muster the strength of purpose to hold high the lantern and strike the bell. Let freedom ring!

LEARNING TO LEARN—ALL OVER AGAIN

There are those who have spoken of the "One Minute Manager" or the "Thirty Second Argument." Few things are so simple. Many years ago I taught a course in the graduate college of the Department of Education at the University of Texas at El Paso. The course was taught "on site" as part of a Teacher Corps project. I recall using a number of texts, including Paolo Freire's *Pedagogy of the Oppressed*. My intent was to get the students to think about the liberating aspects of a broad and penetrating education, as well as how one can experience those "immediate"—existential, if you will—educational opportunities. I attempted to do this with what was then called Curriculum Design: the how and what of the educational delivery system and an organic indebtedness that all of what we know we owe to Nature itself. To some degree I think there was a measure of success. Some of the students became teachers in their own school districts and even administrators.

So, where are we today in the mish-mash of facts, figures, needs, and druthers? Is the educational system better off than it was in the early goings on of our Republic? In some ways yes and in some ways no; learning opportunities abound, yet values seem to have slipped into a situational relativity. Good news on the one hand and disaster on the other.

In a democratic republic you can choose to give away your freedom. All of history's efforts indicate that this is the danger in a democracy; it enables a movement toward mediocrity and then to abject stupidity. I could use the

51

word *ignorance*—and yet I think there is an inherent sense of responsibility that exists in the personhood of the hominid, and it is precisely that sense of personal freedom leading to an informed responsibility that would prevail, must prevail—if we would act with integrity.

The current largess of the federal government is not particularly wise, prudent, or even honest. Ignorant people do not comprehend the challenges and the glorious opportunities of personal freedoms and the subsequent responsibilities. Millennia have been spent in the evolution of and the gaining of these freedoms: freedoms from the vagaries of time and space and the equally important, one might even say concomitant, freedoms to create many things and to project our understandings of ourselves and the world-universe into some knowable and sustainable circumstance.

In both personal and communal ways, the manifestation of selfhood in matters of social, governmental, economic, and religious endeavors has suffered a certain debilitation. Our educational systems have failed to maintain a fidelity to the essential aspects of well-informed members of a voting constituency—a constituency that must participate in the governance and economics as well as the religious well-being of our nation. It has fallen into a state of disrepair.

In all of this too many people have chosen to remain ignorant and we can finally say that now this ignorance is also reflected in the naive faith of the integrity of the Internet. Its omnipresent data cache of inconceivable depth and breadth does indeed reflect as an existential whole—the best and the worst of us all. It really does permeate the totality of the human circumstance. And yes, we also know there are some who live in suppressed and oppressed states, enslaved by governments, religions, and ignorance. And yet, for the first time in human history we (most of us) have the opportunity to grow in our understanding of our human story/stories. In their similitude, there is a certain groundedness that forms the colors of the grand human mosaic— sufficiently available to benefit the sum substance of the human race. There exists a critical mass that—if it would only own with integrity of purpose what it means to be truly human, with a certain magnanimity—could change the course of the human experience.

In this continued conundrum of our shared presence, when we are given the opportunity to choose, again, for ourselves and for our children, we find the "truly innocent, who come and come and come."[27] It is in this "new time" (for the old world has passed away)[28] that we have a greater depth of available knowledge leading to the possibility of an informed understanding, that we must discover a "second religiousness,"[29] a truly righteous ecumenical awareness that opens us to a new reverence of a necessity to express a deeper, a more profound new level of personal and communal integrity. Indeed, a "second religiousness" has become.

It is in this new awareness that we must also assume the essential responsibility to teach each person to recognize the fact that sunrises and sunsets are only ostensibly free. In the face of this organic truth, we must turn our attention to manifesting the integrity of the organic whole into which humanity has been placed. We are it and "it" is us.[30]

ALWAYS HOPE

Always hope! Not because our druthers always end on a high note, but because by some miracle many of them happen at all.

The Washington Prayer Breakfast venue, where Dr. Ben Carson spoke about the fact that Obama Care was going to create a slew of difficult and expensive issues for everyone, was exactly the right venue to seek a deeper understanding and a greater appreciation of the truth in order to give thanks and praise for the ability to apply sufficient reason to have a relationship with the truth. His comments reflected the very essence of our prayers of supplication and adoration. It was well done.

Obama Care is not, as a total piece of legislation, a good thing. It is a terrible thing. Health care is everyone's personal responsibility. It starts with the self and to the degree that we are able, stays with the self. Life's course changes over time. This is something we all inherently know. Being responsible for one's self is an obvious commitment that must be made in anticipation of changes in our health profile and our earning potential as we age. This too is something we all know. To be responsible is to own in an existential fashion the entire profile of the human circumstance in a personal and a societal way. This is the ultimate responsibility of personhood.[31]

MANNERS MATTER

Simply the truth goes a long way in creating an atmosphere of understanding and trust. Showing decorum is a measure of our comprehension of the "other" and demonstrates our "knowledge of, caring for, responsibility for, and respect of" our self and our fellow human beings.[32]

And yet, there are those times when fighting fire with fire is appropriate—a way of controlling the fire by taking away its available destructive fuel. If it has no more fuel it dies. May reason finally prevail in our current media foray! May a return to factual reporting and responsible behavior prevail. And thank God for those few current news outlets who actually approach our information needs with a measured modicum of common sense and integrity.

And so too, driving out the money changers from the temple of government is a creative act—a purposeful effort to remove the unseemly from a holy place. This was not an economic statement. If you have money, use it wisely: "Render unto Caesar what is Caesar's" (taxes that are just). And for us, the postmoderns, we must comment on and expose the waste and fraud, duplicity, and hypocrisy on every front. And as well, we must follow through on the sanctimony of the actions of anyone as we pursue any and all legal, cultural, and moral remedies for unseemly behavior. Prosecute any and all villains! And I feel it now necessary to add, no matter who they are. That is a sad commentary on the current cultural template that many of our fellow countrymen and women espouse.

OBAMA REDUX

Obama has twice donned the mantle of the presidency of the United States. He has attempted twice to assume a cloak that he was and still is unprepared to wear. He has succeeded in winning elections by igniting the age-old bastion of class warfare—the ugly nemesis that bashes the sanctity of each and every one of us—and steals our personal freedoms. He has unabashedly forged ahead with no in-depth understanding of the hidden depths and better aspects of human nature.

Fear-mongering rhetoric delivered with a supercilious quip doesn't get the job done, and this is the only thing that he has offered so far as he nears the end of his second term. This is all he has to offer. I would expect nothing more than what he has delivered. That being the case, I must continue to speak out about this interminably angry adolescent's attitude towards reality: If it is not yours (and he has no clue as to what is ours), then woe be unto you for hurting everyone; it is certainly not something that I would do. He believes that only his way will solve our problems.

His not-so-veiled threats are wearing thin. Messianic hubris reigns! Criminality abounds! Game on!

HOMAGE TO LOUIS L'AMOUR

"And yet, was not the cause of human liberty always every man's trust?

[The movement across this great land of ours] had excited the greed of men, and here in these western lands men were fighting again the age-old struggle for freedom and for civilization, which is one that always must be fought for. The weak, and those unwilling to make the struggle, soon resign their liberties for the protection of powerful men or paid armies; they begin by being protected, they end by being subjected.

Here men had lived, men in an early state of civilization, men organizing their first attempts at a settled community, men thinking out the rules that would give them freedom, for freedom and civilization can exist only where there are laws and agreement.

You cannot allow evil to grow. Each time the good are defeated, or each time they yield, they only cause the forces of evil to grow stronger. Greed feeds greed, and crime grows with success. Our giving up what is ours merely to escape trouble would only create greater trouble for someone else."[33]

This small sample of Louis L'Amour's large volume of work illustrates his reasoned embrace of the wisdom of simple truths. It's no surprise that Mr. L'Amour was the recipient of both the Congressional Gold Medal and the Medal of Freedom.

When I was asked, some years ago, what I thought would ground and enlighten the young, something that would sit right with young seeking minds, for we all start with the curiosity of the young, my suggestions included Louisa May Alcott, Horatio Alger, Jr., Dale Carnegie, and Louis L'Amour, along with the values gleaned from reading some grounded religion, the Ten Commandments, and a knowledge of the manners of a deep and caring culture.

Along with these, all those fundamentals of the literature of the ages, as it pertains to the character of the species, I added a subscription for each and every child to the National Geographic. All of this is to be staged and melded to the reading of any subject a child may have an interest in. Reading is the absolute key to an understanding of one's self and the relationship we have had and have with the world. At this juncture in our species' lengthy history, I would add an in-depth understanding of the role of technology as it relates to human life—all life.

I also believe there is an age-dependency factor with reference to an understanding of all the Internet "stuff." As times have changed, I would now add a continual parsing of the electronic mists and fogs of the technology of the day, with the intent to ground every seeking mind to a recognition, in the onslaught of the age, of only that which complements the heart, body, mind, and soul of the species.

A knowledge of Louis L'Amour's deference to the dictates of Common Sense would add a natural framing reference so essential to the maturation of the young. Parental supervision of the whole process of education is essential and absolute. Adding a familial exercise to the growth and development of the young and their place in humanity's grand journey is an utmost necessity.

From age to age we must follow the same path: the generative "adding on." From childhood to adolescent, from maturing young adult to maturing adult are the only acceptable and functional stages of human development. We must follow a progressive and ascendant participation in a recognition of our own freedoms of self-expression and concomitant responsibility of it all to it all.

TRUTH, FACTS, AND SPENGLER

The following extract is from Oswald Spengler's *Decline of the West*.[34] This is from an abridged edition with a new introduction by H. Stuart Hughes. It makes good reading for those who are so lost in our current garden of circumstances (facts).

> In the historical world there are no ideals, but only facts—no truths, but only facts. There is no reason, no honesty, no equity, no final aim, but only facts and anyone who does not realize this should write books on politics—let him not try to *make* politics. In the real world there are no states [that] build according to ideals, but only state(s) that have *grown*, and these are nothing but living peoples "in form." No doubt it is "the form impressed that living doth itself unfold," but the impress has been that of the blood and beat of a *being*, wholly instinctive and involuntary; and as to the unfolding, if it is guided by the master of politics, it takes the direction inherent in the blood; if by the idealist, that dictated by his own convictions—in other words, the way of nullity.

> The destiny question, for States that exist in reality and not merely in intellectual schemes, is not that of their ideal task or structure, *but that of their inner authority*, which cannot in the long run be maintained by material means, but only by a belief—of friend *and* foe—in their effectiveness. The decisive problems lie, not in the working out of constitutions, but in the organization of a sound working government; not in

the distribution of political rights according to "just" principles (which at bottom are simply the idea that a *class* forms of its own legitimate claims), but in the efficient pulse of the whole (efficient in the sense that the play of muscle and sinew is efficient when an extended racehorse nears the winning-post), in that rhythm which attracts even strong genius into syntony; not, lastly, in any world-alien moral, but in the steadiness, sureness and superiority of political leadership. The more self-evident all these things are, the less is said or argued about them; the more fully matured the State, the higher the standing, the historical capacity and therefore the Destiny of the Nation. State-majesty, sovereignty, is a life-symbol of the first order. It distinguishes *subjects* and *objects*. Strength of leadership, which comes to expression in the clear separation of these two factors, is the unmistakable sign of the life-force in a political unity—so much so that the shattering of existing authority (for example, by the supporters of an opposed constitutional ideal) almost always results not in this new party's making itself the subject of domestic policy, but in the whole nation's becoming the object of alien policy—and not seldom forever.

* * *

There is no best, or true, or right State that could possibly be actualized according to plan. Every State that emerges in history exists as it is but once and for a moment; the next moment it has, unperceived, become different, whatever the rigidity of its legal-constitutional crust. Therefore, words like republic, absolutism, and democracy mean something different in every instance, and what turns them into catchwords is their use as definite concepts by philosophers and ideo-

61

logues. A history of States is physiognomic and not systematic. Its business is not to show how "humanity" advances to the conquest of its eternal rights, to freedom and equality, to the evolving of a super-wise and super-just State, but to describe the political units that really exist in the fact-world, how they grow and flourish and fade and how they are really nothing but actual life "in form."

And it is this that must govern our thinking in our current circumstance. These ideas are a backdrop for our understanding of our own way of life as we attempt some fundamental grasp of our moving picture. We appear, we surge, or we crawl, from the arms of Evolution's efforts. To this we must adhere and we must always bow to Nature's holy drift. While we can say with some assurance, "once having been, always will be" in some historical factual, faithful sense, it may be that in some conscious sense of self we may not quite be able to grasp the complete meaning of our conscious selves. Yet we still may become part of an ineffable whole that cradles us and give us that sense of oneness in the One to the one. This bespeaks an absolute dedication to a purpose that benefits us all.

WHY IS IT THAT …

Why is it that so many of us see only scatter-grams of the enclaves of wisdom, depravity, and ignorance in the accumulations of our deep reflections, and focus too much on the raw bestiality of man?

One would think that from the passions of our "worst and best" we would have shed the "less than" and put on the coat of the "more than" of our kind. The distillation of our goodness—kindness to our self, family, and tribe—has episodically shown itself, and yet the lingerings of madness continue. The sway between extremes, the gentle sweetness of honey and the bitter herb, has been all that many could see.

Hatred and expedience has led us to slaughter both others and our own. In cold blood and hot, we have sinned against us all. One would have hoped the journey had been long enough for us to grow up and out, away from the destruction of our kind and the treasures of the ages. But no, the creatures of the darkness yet roam. Greatness and malevolence is carried in our minds and hearts. It has been written: "We know so little. We pretend so much."[35]

We have yet to learn enough to read the tea leaves of our times and our own kind. The genes, the hearts, the minds of the species, they all carry the written and unwritten codes of conduct that have birthed the saints and the crazies of history—a history that was, is now, and forever shall be.

Still some of us make, in all of this, vain and real attempts to parse the good from the bad, the mercy and the justice in the softness and the hard. We try to mete out both in the hours of our lives, bounded moments, in which we love and hate in a time we like to call our own. We even speak about an infinitude of heaven and hell, when deep down inside we know the limits of our lives and those lives that spring from loins and wombs. We also, nonetheless, bequeath to a progeny of similitude, over which and ostensibly for whom we have waxed and waned in our less-than-righteous commitments, eternal truths swirling in the crucible of humankind.

A PERCEPTION OF OUR PLACE IN TIME

It has been written, "Iraq—The Last War."[36] There will supposedly never again be huge armies "in the field" facing each other—unless we call the global moment a "battle-field." And a case could be made for that. And yet I also think that what we need is a perspectival orientation that takes into consideration the historical presence of our species on the planet earth.

Our historical behavior ranges from, among other things, the retributional to the sacrificial, from the ideological and religious to the political, all of which form a part of the human repertoire of behavior.

The difficult issues for the foreseeable future will be sectarian violence and the mundane. There will also be all kinds of forms of brutal ideological confrontations and factions—actions precipitating a broad range of behavior affecting the arenas of the intellectual, physical, emotional, and spiritual. This will continue at some level forever, and will only substantially dissipate and learn to adhere to a vital focus when sufficient numbers of people realize there is enough room for everyone on the globe. A mutual knowledge of, a caring for, a responsibility for, and a respect of, are what we need.

There have always been seasons of disaffection and it seems that, although to some degree these various activities will continue, human life will also continue to take all of the four seasons to accomplish the tasks of cultural change and development as we mature as a species. A bursting spring will be followed by a hot summer, a cooling fall, a waiting winter, and finally a new spring will come to pass, with the seeds from the previous seasons germinating and driving roots ever deeper into the fertile pockets of old cultures where insufficient openness prevailed, and yet sufficient ingredients were distilled and held ready for the next maturing season, a season for the ripening of new fruit, new potentials, new creativity in every realm: the intellectual, physical, emotional, and last but not least, the spiritual would also grow and develop.

Still these ever-renewing seasons will also continue to bring spontaneous expiational acts of violence—wolf pack and lone wolf mentalities committing acts of unimaginable brutality expressed from some incomprehensible and archaic sub-consciousness to the mentally ill—and these will always be with us. Dismemberments and the wanton loss of the lives of the unborn, the young, the middle aged and the elderly, all brothers and sisters, daughters and sons of the species will horrify us all, and this carnage will raise its ugly head again and again. These bursts of violent acts that would have been impossible before today or the day before yesterday (for the old has passed away) will spill across the landscape. The facts of human life, encompassing in their wholeness the full spectrum of behavior, will also continue to spill forth from every segment of society.

There is always on nature's side what seems to be a darkness that brings new light. The astrophysics of our understanding always hearkens back to, or ahead to, the cataclysmic. It is true that nature—though quiescent most of the time—can suddenly be devastating, and that devastation can have long-range social effects for the human family. And in the human realm, acts of violent degradations on other members of our human family can scar the generations caught up in the seasonal and cataclysmic changes. Indeed, it may take generations for the wounds to heal sufficiently for a healthy "critical mass" to provide sufficient stability and focus for families and individuals to mature and share a loving presence with others of their kind. This has always come to pass.

This intermittent brutal intentionality will not stop the natural effervescence of "freedom rising" in the human spirit. Nature's greatest recognizable gift from the evolutionary ages is freedom itself—that fulfilling of innate aspirations as owned and expressed in human life, indeed in all life, the very whole of existence.

Freedom speaks to every single capable individual as a profound responsibility of selfhood and personhood—these are unique manifestations of the universe's efforts of sharing itself with all other conscious selves and indeed everything in the universe. And for those less informed or less willing, it also speaks for those phasing moments of conception when the helpless need our help, when simple and gallant acts of human valor say "Yes!" to life, all life. When we will finally humbly and conscientiously assume responsibility to the degree we are able, for the whole human race.

This obvious fact—the expression of freedom by the human spirit—testifies to the inherent movement of growth and development. Without waxing too poetic or lauding magnanimously, one could say life itself is a salvific exercise.

It must also be added that it is not just the crescent of Arab nations in the Middle East and the Islamic countries of Africa and Asia that struggle; it is also each and every enclave in every phasing place in the world that is trying to serve the many who are struggling to appreciate and find a place for themselves in the great human epic.

Mention must be made here also of the historic, accumulated paranoia of Russia and China, in which they feel that they will be put upon by the rest of the world, and while they fumblingly attempt to gain sufficient understanding of the current slaughters in the real world, they hinder the progress of each and every manifestation of freedom in the whole of which they are a part.

As the human species yearns and learns to move forward from the cavalier attitudes of the adolescent, we must go on to mature into the heroic commitments of conscious selves shouldering our share of the focused efforts of the Divine Plan. We must acknowledge the truth of what we know now and live with our awareness of those deep and profound acclamations echoing through the halls of Nature's efforts: Pay attention or die! Let freedom ring!

THANK YOU OBAMA

The petulant, arrogant, angry adolescent has given this great country of ours a wake-up call of the utmost importance. "We the people" of this great nation have fallen into a somnambulant state of forgotten, disregarded, cynical, and lost responsibility.

In that famous modality of what is truly human—the think, say, do, of our most mature recognizable paradigm—we have become less than deserving of our own freedoms and their concomitant responsibilities.

The trail of deceit and political arrogance has run full circle. We now have sufficient information to see what has been attempted by this administration and the consequences of those immature actions. Now is the time to send a clear message that elections have consequences and the people are beginning to awaken. We have Andrew McCarthy's deftly written book, *Faithless Execution—Building the Political Case for Obama's Impeachment*, Ben Shapiro's text *The People vs. Barack Obama—The Criminal Case Against the Obama Administration*, and David Limbaugh's *Crimes Against Liberty—An Indictment of President Obama*. All of these set down in no uncertain terms the case for impeachment of this floundering and incompetent president.

We must now follow through with our personal and national commitments to the documents that frame the intent and purpose of this great nation. We need, the nation needs, and the world needs a dedicated commitment to the well-being of those sacred callings that shape our lives and the lives of all those who seek an expression of the fundamental precepts that speak to the very soul of humankind.

BALTIMORE

Only a tiny glint of a reflection
– hints of trouble.
There is a shuddering in my soul.
How thin the water on the land?
Most has been wicked away.
Should we be concerned
that it will all be gone
leaving only barren ground?
Too little have we done
to preserve the sacredness of Nature.
We have ridden rough shod
over her breasts and shoulders:
desecrated vales,
squandered time.
We have bred wolf pups
and abandoned them to themselves,
have failed ourselves and future generations.
Woe be unto us, the U.S.
Smoldering remnants
of a once vibrant culture
slip into time,
leaving only tracks of decadence
scattered in the shoals
of our forgotten
and abandoned responsibilities.
We see the crops of Baltimore
raging in the streets.
Must we only stand stupefied and watch?
Are there are no leaders left?

THE BALTIMORE SYNDROME

Baltimore is a medium-sized city (600,000±) where some hundreds of rioters and looters destroyed/caused some 9 million dollars in damages. In other words, perhaps 500–1,000 individuals, approximately 0.001 percent of the population, created a disturbance that affected not just a city or a state, but a nation, and as well sent a message to the world. This should give us pause.

Ostensibly, the death of a known criminal and again ostensibly, the death caused by the local police, were the sparks that ignited the social unrest that caused the disturbance. It is prudent to recall and understand that there was a before, a during, and an after that belong to this event. All of which were laden with fungible facts, facts that depend upon a point of view, a bias, a blend of truths and falsehoods.

How is one to sort out sufficient information to make some reasonable assessments as to causes, faults, and facts?

There are times when facts may appear to be self-evident. And yet, in the real world, reasonable people can disagree. The proverbial "rush to judgment" by a broad spectrum of any given group has been and will continue to be a problem. In the statistical curves of crazies and saints, ignorant and well-informed, young and old, racial and cultural enclaves of minorities, and integrated homogeneous groups of the majorities, we stand in a present as recipients of past efforts and future hopes. We all stand somewhere along the "statistical curve" close to or far away from the center.

Must there, of necessity, always be a clash among all of these life participants?

I really don't think so, and yet there seems to be, more often than not, some strong feelings that are oppositional; one might even say the difference is always poised to be confrontational. The generational gaps, the racial and cultural divides, class differences, malevolent individuals, and different histories always dispose. One could hope that we would learn to seek the complementary.

The history of the species records these gaps, divides, differences, and evil as having been sufficient to precipitate for long periods of time the species' machinations, unrest, difficulties, and accomplishments. And yet in today's world with some 8 billion individuals on the planet we have a preponderance of peace among the vast majority of peoples. Why is it that some still choose stupidity, ignorance, and violence?

And why is it that along the roads of war and peace and more war and peace there have been these waxings and wanings that still diminish pursuits of peace-loving activities? There is a long gentle road of a progressive and ascendant movement of humankind that has produced truly incredible accomplishments. Indeed, we have continued to move toward a greater and greater understanding leading to convivial circumstances for most of the time for most of the world's people.

However, we cannot ignore the fact that there are bad people, evil is alive and well in the human family, and this necessitates an eternal vigilance. In this vein we cannot be so naive that we don't see the professional rabble rousers, anarchists, and criminals of every ilk that can and do take advantage of the mob behavior of the moment.[37]

This brings us back to the current unrest in Baltimore in the twent-first century. A lot of questions surge to the surface of our thinking: How could such a small group of individuals wreak such havoc? Who were they and why would they do such a hideous thing? Why were they allowed to rage on? And what were the rest of the people of Baltimore doing and thinking while the destruction was taking place?

Well ... the simple answer may be that unattended children or adolescents can be very mischievous, especially when they have not been taught respect for other people and their property. There are many other reasons that may shed light on our understanding. All adolescents are rambunctious, but not all adolescents are inherently destructive and dangerous. So what are some of the conditions that would precipitate such behavior? Isolation, ignorance, boredom, stupidity, acquiescing, malevolence, copycatting, abandonment—we could create a long list. This begs a question: Why would there be so many (there will always be a few and this necessitates a constant policing activity) who exhibit some or all of these circumstances?

Immediately our minds should turn to their families and their surrounding circumstances. Was there sufficient loving care and supervision in their families? Did their surrounding circumstance manifest progressive movement of others toward opportunities for a growth and development that could take advantage of opportunities for advancement in achievements, and the expressions of dreams for a greater and deeper opportunity to satisfy those dreams? Were there criminal types that mirrored a false success?

74

We are a wandering and wondering species and if stymied, or stifled, we "break out," sometimes in very destructive ways. We need to identify the specific prevailing conditions that contributed to and produced such problematic thinking and behavior in Baltimore.

Was it a lack of familial security, the effects of the values of a dominant culture, a deep and abiding ignorance, a fundamental confusion in understanding the realities of life, evil itself, or all or some of the above?

The facts on the ground dictate that it was some of all of the above. Whose responsibility are these children, these young adolescents, these thugs, these criminals, these malcontents? In what state of being do we find them? Are they capable of positive dreams and a desire to manifest them in some equanimical fashion in some actual world?

Again, the facts on the ground draw our attention: some do and some do not manage to transition from childhood to adolescent, to maturing young adults, to maturing adults on some progressive and positive track. There obviously were, in parts of the city of Baltimore, prevailing circumstances that led to insufficient maturity and loss of hope for the future. The spectrum of reality always ranges from benign to malignant activity. For these reasons we need to police ourselves by ourselves and with others.

In the familial and communal context there was insufficient love and leadership to provide for growth, opportunity, or policing activity. Impoverished single-parent families find great difficulty in providing that committed union of decorum, supervision, and aspiration. Couple this with incompetent civic leadership and a lack of surrounding opportunities along with the local and imported thugs and you have a fuse waiting to be lit. When a person's expectations—especially those of instant gratification by the young and the criminal elements along with the local and imported thugs who do not know how to move in some committed and reasonable fashion in a here and now time frame toward their chosen goals—do not provide the desired outcomes, there will be disruptions and destruction. And we must always remember that all actions have consequences.

Is there a place in all of this for an inherent blameless attitude towards those involved in civic unrest? Not hardly! To let anyone incite and rage on and maim and destroy was a stupid response by any measure of comprehension. Every rational person must bear a measure of personal responsibility for their own actions. For this we have laws and those that enforce those laws.

It must be asked, how did we end up with such a cesspool of cynics preying upon each other and others? And to those who just see numbers, remember that many of them choose to be where they are: In prison and in dysfunctional enclaves of like-minded people.

In the human family there are generations and cross generations that exude a full spectrum of behaviors ranging from heroic to despicable. There is always a need for those few heroes when a few can and must save the many.

Advice for Baltimore (and the entire nation): Circulate petitions to recall all incompetent elected city, county, state, and federal officials that had anything to do with Baltimore's failures. Fire all incompetent appointed bureaucrats such as the police commissioner and police chief. Review the school superintendent and principals of all schools, and many of the teachers in the city schools may be woefully inadequate for the task at hand. Although it is not their responsibility to make up for chronic deficits in the social whole, it is their responsibility to demand the essentials of decorum and to maintain a serious commitment in their respective endeavors. We must all remember that teaching the young is a sacred endeavor.

Incompetence does not deliver responsible actions. Pass a city statute that requires all future candidates for public office to publish a personal manifesto (no one could any longer hide behind any party or affiliation) of what they stand for and what they will spend their time and energy doing. Where every penny will come from for their agenda and how it will be spent. And we must publish the outcomes of every penny spent. Accountability is critical— and it cannot be had from a relativistic insipidness or from naive thinking.

Don't wait for any outside help! We all must come to bear the cost of freedom writ large! Get smart! Get honest! Do the right things! Start now!

HOW IMPORTANT IS THIS MOMENT?

This moment is of supreme importance. The fates of nations and of the world hang in the balance; even worse, some are on a precipice, and going over this precipice will create untold suffering for the entire global population.

An omnipresent existential choice always stands before us: Maintain a fidelity to that oneness of being that makes us who and what we are. It impinges on the honor of history, on the execution of the present, and on the portfolio of the future. Actions have value; they matter.

In the latest edition of his very successful book *Things That Matter*, Charles Krauthammer adds a few columns dedicated to parsing the actions of Obama and his administration. He cites the facts as well as the consequences of these actions, some of which he considers to be illegal. These issues must not be left unsettled. If there is just cause, Obama should be impeached.

Meanwhile Andrew McCarthy cites seven articles that he considers impeachable offenses in his book *Faithless Execution: Building the Political Case for Obama's Impeachment*. He notes that "Impeachment is a political remedy, not a legal one; it is a question of the public's will to remove the president, not a matter of whether impeachable offenses can be proved." The truth is that they must be proven, at least in the hearts and minds of the governed, in order for any action to be taken.

Recognizing that the process of impeachment must be an expression of the will of the people, an agreement on some "high crime," I find that a realization can come when one gathers sufficient facts and proceeds to a connection of those facts to given circumstances and given individuals. I see this in the articles by McCarthy and I make the connection with the office of the president of the United States and with the collusion of some in his administration.

The odd thing is that those in the administration could be found guilty of obstructing justice which is a crime punishable by law and yet the president must be impeached for the same crime. Why is it that the same thing can be done by two different people and one can be found guilty before a court of law and the other must be impeached for the same reason? Is one above the law and the other subject to the law? And if the Constitution is the "law of the land" why couldn't both be prosecuted for having transgressed the Constitution and obstructed justice? I hope that none of us will ever have to read the words: "He should have been impeached." Or, "They should have been convicted." What lily-livered persons would take joy in those words by saying, "Well he wasn't was he?" Where are those patriots who will put honor and justice before all else?

We understand that the United States was established with three coequal branches of government and that we must maintain their separate but equal status or we would have a perennial political farce. (A case could be made that we are having that anyway.)

We also know that "we the people" are the fourth coequal branch of government and we, as a super majority (as represented by two-thirds of the Senate), must move the Senate to carry out the impeachment process. In today's world how would a two-thirds majority manifest itself? Would it be in an interminable number of polls that can be argued forever in the press, in the less-than-expedient courts, in the talk shows of the day and elsewhere? This would lead to a stalemate, a crisis of stagnation, and finally a poll-weary citizenry who would just drop all interest in a crisis of static bickering. Their incredibly short attention span would merely turn to the entertainment venues of the day and as automatons they would march their way to serfdom.

Where are the courageous souls, or groups of courageous souls, that can raise a voice and begin that cresting wave of truth and push for a resolution to impeach and find guilty those who have sworn to uphold the "laws of the land," those who have intentionally failed miserably through intent and incompetence?

Our President, our Congress, and our Supreme Court have made this country the laughing stock of the world and have caused the deaths and sufferings of vast numbers of innocent people. They have turned a blind eye and a cold-stone heart to all the citizens of this nation and the world. And if we think we deserve better, we need to be the ones who take this country back from the functionaries and bureaucrats who don't have a clue as to the true magnificence of this freedom-loving species. We need to send a very clear message to every person in our floundering great republic and to the world that this malevolence and incompetence will not stand.

I here add my voice to that cresting wave and call for the courts, the House, and the Senate to be put on notice that this process must begin with all the dispatch we can muster. We must send a message to the entire country and to the world that "we the people" of this nation will not shrink back and do nothing. We must immediately take over the reins of government and set a new course that adheres to the Constitution of the United States of America. This president and his administration have done more harm to the fabric of this nation than any other previous president or administration. We cannot wait, nor should we, for the next election. We have the facts and we have the means.

We must send a message to those liberals (who are anything but liberal) and those progressives (who are anything but honest) about the nature of the species: We are that freedom-seeking soul that has taken eons to manifest sufficient infrastructure to thwart the demonic nature of human power that corrupts as it grows in (ostensible) power. We must stay the course.

Impeach now! Convict! Let freedom ring! Move on!

A BRIEF AFTERWORD

Thomas Friedman and Michael Mandelbaum have said it—
not all, but enough—in their widely read text *That Used to
Be Us: How America Fell Behind in the World it Invented
and How We Can Come Back.*

That fact is that we cannot "come back." We must move
ahead in our current world, according to the wherewithal of
the present. According to Friedman and Mandelbaum:

> The central question in our national political life today
> should be: How do we create enough jobs and eco-
> nomic growth to pay off our debts and pass on a higher
> standard of living to our children without despoiling
> the environment, while also supplying the global lead-
> ership that the world needs?[38]

And:

> Neither of America's two major parties seems able to
> address in serious fashion the challenges the country
> confronts. Their political philosophies are worlds
> apart, and neither outlook is suitable for the present
> moment. The Democrats act as if government is the
> solution to all of America's difficulties; the Republi-
> cans act as if government is the cause of all of them.
> The Democrats behave as if virtually every program
> the government created in the twentieth century is
> perfect and cannot be changed in any way; the Repub-
> licans seek to send the country back to the nineteenth
> century, before any of those programs existed. Neither

approach will give the country the policies it needs to succeed in the decades to come.[39]

Well said! The facts are well known. It is the hearts and souls needed to accept them and to act upon them that are wanting.

Notes

[1] See Andrew McCarthy, *Faithless Execution—Building the Political Case for Obama's Impeachment* (Encounter Books, 2014).

[2] This list is from the Psycholinguistic chapter in *The Game of Life: A Player's Manual for Executives and Others.* http://amzn.to/fgeCeV

[3] See "Thank You Obama" in this collection.

[4] Part One is in *Sign Posts V.*

[5] "Fields of Sacrifice," from *Always Extolling: A Collection.* http://amzn.to/gpHPRB

[6] Teilhard de Chardin was a French Jesuit paleontologist whose many writings present a religious progressive and ascending life expression. See especially *The Phenomenon of Man,* and also *The Divine Milieu* as well as *The Future of Man, Christianity and Evolution,* and *The Activation of Energy.*

[7] From *The Phenomenon of Man,* by Teilhard de Chardin.

[8] This poem first appeared in *Sign Posts Volume V* and again in *Still Water: A Collection.* I think it bears repeating. http://amzn.to/gpHPRB

[9] *La Vida es Sueño Segismundo,* by Pedro Calderón de la Barca.

[10] I cannot remember who said this! But it seems worth repeating here.

[11] From *Still Water: A Collection,* by Don Davison. http://amzn.to/gpHPRB

[12] See the trilogy of poems on the subject of Ignorance in *Sign Posts V.* http://amzn.to/fgeCeV

[13] From *Still Water, A Collection,* by Don Davison. http://amzn.to/gpHPRB

[14] From *I And Thou,* a classic philosophical work by Martin Buber that also addresses religious, relational ethics (Touchstone, 1971).

[15] George Steiner, *The Death of Tragedy* (Yale University Press, 1996).

[16] You may be interested in "Let Me Speak!," a poem in *Pebbles on the Shore, A Collection.* http://amzn.to/gpHPRB

[17] From *La Celestina,* by Castilian author Fernanado de Rojas (Penguin Classics, 2009).

[18] Rule Two from *The Game of Life: A Player's Manual for Executives and Others,* by Don Davison. http://amzn.to/fOrqEi

[19] These five poems are from *Through the Swamps of Time: A Collection,* by Don Davison. http://amzn.to/gpHPRB

[20] From Oswald Spengler's *The Decline of the West,* an abridged edition with a new introduction by H. Stuart Hughes (Oxford University Press, New York, 1991).

[21] Ibid.

[22] Both cultural quotes offer examples of a healthy dose of truth from a bank of common sense that adheres to each and every piece of known history.

[23] From Plato's dialog *Phaedo*.

[24] The Holy Bible, Duay-Rheims Challoner version.

[25] See *The Game of Life: A Player's Manual for Executives and Others*, by Don Davison. http://amzn.to/fOrqEi

[26] The following article was written on the threshold of the twentieth century by L. P. Jacks, for *The Journal of Adult Education*. How long does it take us to learn some of the most important information for the continuation of our human presence? "The quality of the spiritual food that mankind gets for its soul is strictly dependent on the way it goes about the business of earning the daily bread that feeds its body. If the breadwinning part of its business contributes nothing to its spiritual nourishment, the soul of civilization will die of famine, all social reforms, political philosophies and religious revivals notwithstanding; while the drugs, stimulants, and appetizers made use of to keep it alive will only hasten the process of spiritual decay. In this article I am pleading for the continuity of things. Breadwinning and soul-saving are not two independent operations—most assuredly not when the soul of a civilization is in question. They form a single and continuous operation, called material, if we look at it from one end, spiritual if we look at it from the other. A civilization saves its soul by the way it wins its daily bread. And I have no hesitation in saying that the chief reason why the various soul-saving enterprises now in being are yielding such meager results lies in the general overlooking of this elementary and everlasting truth ... A type of education based on this vision of continuity is, obviously, the outstanding need of our times. Its outlook will be lifelong. It will look upon the industry of civilization as the great "continuation school" for intelligence and for character, and its object will be, not merely to fit men and women for the specialized vocations they are to follow, but also to animate the vocations themselves with ideals of excellence appropriate to each. At the risk of seeming fantastic I will venture to say that the final objective of the New Education is the gradual transformation of the industry of the world into the university of the world; *in other words, the gradual bringing about of a state of things in which 'breadwinning' and 'soul saving' instead of being, as now, disconnected and often opposed operations, shall become a single and continuous operation*." (Italics added.)

[27] "Reap the Wind" was first published in *Always Extolling: A Collection*, by Don Davison. http://amzn.to/gpHPRB

[28] The Book of Revelation, from the Bible.

[29] See *The Decline of the West*, by Oswald Spengler (Oxford University Press, 1991).

[30] See "To Dream," in *Sign Posts V*. http://amzn.to/fgeCeV

[31] You may wish to read the two essays on health care in *Sign Posts II* and III. http://amzn.to/fgeCeV Also see the wearing of one's personhood in *The Game of Life: A Player's Manual for Self and Others*, by Don Davison. http://amzn.to/fOrqEi

[32] See *The Art of Loving*, by Erich Fromm (Perennial Library, 1974).

[33] **Louis L'Amour, names of his works etc., direct quotes.**

[34] Spengler, *The Decline of the West*, abridged edition with introduction by H. Stuart Hughes (Oxford University Press, New York, 1991)

[35] "Species Lost," in *Through the Swamps of Time: A Collection*, by Don Davison. http://amzn.to/gpHPRB

[36] In *Sign Posts I*.
http://amzn.to/fgeCeV

[37] This is why *manners matter*. It helps us to keep closed the doors of opportunity for those so inclined to social disruptions. "Just say no!" must be followed by "Just don't do!" Behavior matters. Decorum must prevail.

[38] Thomas L. Friedman and Michael Mandelbaum, *That Used to Be Us: How America Fell Behind in the World it Invented and How We Can Come Back* (Picador, reprint edition, 2012), pp. xv.

[39] Ibid., p. 350.